An opinionated guide to

WINE
LONDON

CW01496998

Written by
TOM HOWELLS

Planque (no.24)

INFORMATION IS DEAD.
LONG LIVE OPINION.

Why bother reading a guidebook when everything you could want to know about wine is available online? You've wasted your money.

No! This isn't just more information; it's straight-forward, simple opinion. The world of wine can be snooty and impenetrable. Thankfully, London's wine scene is not. This city is overflowing with fresh, fun places to enjoy a glass (or bottle), and this is your unashamedly bold and opinionated guide to the best of them – whether you want something Old World, New World or out-of-this-world.

Martin
Co-founder, Hoxton Mini Press

Above and opposite: Cadet (no.16)

Bar Levan (no.41)
Opposite: Hector's (no.15)

Top Cuvée (no.32)
Opposite: Lulu's (no.45)

GRAPE EXPECTATIONS

Boozing in London is a multifaceted joy: a landscape of rarefied and delectable poisons of all stripes and, crucially, a consummate wine drinker's city.

As an occasionally penniless food journalist subsisting on PR handouts (and the kind of man who has, quite delightedly, quaffed €3 flagons of indeterminate Carrefour plonk on numerous bicycle tours), I'd always been of the mindset that, like pizza and gelato before it, even crap wine was a better-than-average comestible. London has changed that thinking (a bit).

The scope of good drinking here is head-razing. This is a town overflowing with dedicated bars, brilliantly curated restaurant lists, convivial bottle shops, proactive importers, vineyards in striking distance of the city and even a few urban winemakers, offering everything from palette-smashing, low-intervention (a.k.a., natural or *natty*) funk to premier-cru French reds at prices that'd make a minor aristocrat wince.

'Traditionally' made wine still abounds (that is, industrially made bottles that have had additives, chemicals and preservatives added along the way), but it's impossible to understand the sodden landscape without taking into account the wild bloom of natural and low-intervention wines. My own immersion came with weekly visits to the late, lamented Terroirs in Charing Cross in the 2010s, but natural wine has proliferated into ubiquity. Beginning with extant 'second wave' pioneers like Sager + Wild (no.28), Brawn (no.26) and 40 Maltby Street (no.50) and on into the current, fecund crop of places like Dan's (no.17), Bar Levan (no.41), Quality Wines (no.11) etc. ad infinitum. Saying that, almost every venue in this book, even if not dogmatically natural, focuses on wines made with high regard for its terroir, often following organic or biodynamic principles. For the discerning, an eye on sustainability is the new normal.

Given the heady provision of the stuff in London, this book is but a snapshot of the scene. There are conspicuous omissions, but there's something here for everyone. Casual, super-chic spots in which to neck beamy (light) pét-nats or tumblers of sunny grüner? To Hector's (no.15), Lulu's (no.45) and Top Cuvée (no.32) with you. More in the market for sloshing back a little claret, with something gutsy to soak it up? It's St. JOHN (no.9) or Cloth (no.3). Neighbourhood emporia where you're as likely to form friendships as you are cataclysmic hangovers? Salthouse in Brockley (no.47), or Joyau (no.25) in Forest Gate. A deep dive into the esoteric reaches of a particular country? Head to Polentina (no.36) for Italy and Newcomer (no.34) for Austria. The list goes on (and on, and on).

I'll be the first to admit I'm not a WSET-accredited expert or sommelier-in-waiting – just a thirsty gannet who knows what they like. I suspect you are too. Pop a cork or cap and get sipping.

Tom Howells
London, 2024

BEST FOR...

Visiting on a budget

Tap wine is the MO at Borough Wines (no.43), and the sustainable approach keeps things hyper-cheap. Less budget than bargain, but the cellar at The Drapers Arms (no.14) is a trove of wicked bottles with insanely democratic markups.

Late nights

In thrall to both Parisian *caves* and the beanie-wearing, moustachioed caché of its postcode, Peckham's Bar Levan (no.41) is lively past midnight on weekends. The Pelican (no.54) is equally spirited, albeit with a far more west London crowd.

Rare finds

Few contemporary spots have the curatorial heft of Noble Rot (no.1), and the upper reaches of its by-the-glass *carte* is full of bucket-list gems. Planque (no.24) was born of its owner's heaving wine collection, jewels of which are still occasionally uncorked for sale.

Enlightening tastings

Nothing beats wandering the verdant pastures of Tillingham vineyard (no.63) – except getting half-cut on its wares while you learn the secrets of natural viniculture. Back in London, shop/shack Wingnut (no.23) holds insightful Thirsty Thursdays, tasting their small yield and super-alternative bottles.

Unusual surroundings

Fancy swooning, sunset skyline views with your pét-nat? Forza Wine (no. 37), sitting high above southeast London, is your gal. Across the Thames, the dank cave at Gordon's (no.5) is a weirdly alluring date-night staple.

Hipster caché

With its waves of matte formica, artistic pâté en croûte and blissful airy aura, Cadet (no.16) has unsurpassed cool credentials. Clapton's 107 (no.21), meanwhile, remains the natty wine bar *du decade* (new nomenclature notwithstanding).

Natural wine newbies

It may be in deep King's Cross, but Half Cut Market (no.13) is a highly laid-back and approachable spot to get acquainted with the new styles. Otherwise, there's always something new to learn at 40 Maltby Street (no.50), Gergovie's offshoot bar.

Community interest

Sociable Acton hub Vindinista (no.57) is a place where they actually do pride themselves on knowing the locals' names. Going east, Joyau (no.25) is a nexus for Forest Gate's bijous young families, with strong neighbourhood vibes.

Old-school charm

Both an oenophile's dream and London's most romantically antiquated restaurant, Andrew Edmunds (no.58) is a tied-on Soho classic for a reason. Le Beaujolais (no.4) is maniacally Gallic, but with similar place-out-of-time appeal.

1

NOBLE ROT

Holy Grail pours from the world's best wine mag

It's tough to play down just what impact Noble Rot's Chin Chin house wine – a zesty, lightly acidic vinho verde – has had on London's more youthful wine-sloshing scene (not least as inspiration for umpteen hipster-baiting Hackney memes). But this micro-empire – comprising three restaurants, an importer (Keeling Andrew & Co), two shops (Shrine to the Vine, no.20) and a colourful magazine that's almost single-handedly destuffified and democratised the world of wine writing – is so much more than one bottle. Splendid food aside (the turbot braised in oxidised Bâtard-Montrachet is a staple), the book-sized *carte* at its claret-red Bloomsbury flagship restaurant is essential reading for any self-respecting wine buff, with some high-end, bucket-list bangers available by the glass.

51 Lamb's Conduit Street, WC1N 3NB
Nearest station: Russell Square
Other locations: Soho, Mayfair
noblerot.co.uk

2
LEROY

Neo-bistro in a Shoreditch byway

A wine list, explains sommelier Ed Thaw, is a little like a guitar: commonplace, but utterly distinct depending on who's playing it. It's a winsome credo exemplified at Leroy – the neon-signed, backstreet bistro that he co-founded in 2018. The list has grown substantially since its inception, now numbering 450 bottles that span myriad countries and regions. Whether natural, 'less natural' or classic, the philosophy is simply to sell great wines, wherever they're from. They've no time for homogenous dogmatism, either: Thaw is vocally averse to eschewing the old-school classics for the sake of hipster caché, so those with the proclivity for blasting £1,300 on an '82 Margaux will be well served.

18 Phipp Street, EC2A 4NU
Nearest station: Shoreditch High Street
leroyshoreditch.com

3

CLOTH

Old world allure from two industry experts

A back-alley warren of dusky green dining rooms, gilt-framed oils, ivory cutlery and a congenial, candlelit atmosphere, modern European restaurant Cloth is perfectly in keeping with its historic locale. Situated in a Grade II-listed Smithfield corner spot, in a row that survived the Great Fire, it's the work of one star chef, Tom Hurst, and two wine mavens. Penzer Wines' Joe Haynes specialises in small producers from France, Italy, Germany and Austria, while Ben Butterworth is an expert in dynamic vignerons from the Bordelaise region. The wine list is a canny melding of interests both classic and leftfield – whether traditional method lambruscos (miles from sweet holiday dreck), flinty Luxembourgish rieslings or citrussy (and faintly petrol-smelling) long-aged German mosel.

Cloth Fair, EC1A 7JQ
Nearest station: Barbican
clothrestaurants.com

4

LE BEAUJOLAIS

Trop Gallic gem with a titular focus

Doing the hardcore, low-lit Gallic thing since way back in 1972, Le Beaujolais – tucked away on a Charing Cross side street, lurching distance from The Ivy – is a place-out-of-time institution, awash with *classique* bent-wood seating, hanging tankards and dress ties, a sea of Gauloises-yellowed ephemera and, naturally, a gargantuan cheese selection for nibbling. ('We want our guests,' explains co-owner Terence Darcel understatedly, 'to feel like they're in France.') The bar is compact and the all-French cellar likewise. Wines from Burgundy, Bordeaux and the Rhône abound, and, naturally, the ten villages of the top-tier 'Crus Beaujolais' designation are all represented. Hardly *à la mode*, but pray it never changes.

25 Litchfield Street, WC2H 9NJ
Nearest station: Leicester Square
lebeaujolais.london

5

GORDON'S

The capital's oldest, dampest wine bar (est.1890)

Are you a true Londoner if you've not been on a damp (literally) squib of a first date at Gordon's? That's rhetorical: Villiers Street's finest is an institution, its archaic, liver-coloured frontage the portal to a gloriously dank, subterranean bolthole adorned with age-weathered wooden panelling, barrels of port and sherry propped behind the bar, chalkboard menus and faded royal newspaper clippings. The list is almost unreconstructedly Old World, with few exceptions (a cabernet, shiraz and viognier blend from southern India's Nandi Hills, anyone?); the food – cheese, baguettes, cold pies – mere ballast for the plonk. The thronging summer terrace is delightful but securing a seat in the candlelit 'cave' room is an inimitable London experience.

47 Villiers Street, WC2N 6NE
Nearest station: Embankment
gordonswinebar.com

6

LADY OF THE GRAPES

Female-focused wines

With it's blood-red frontage and burnished neo-bistro interiors, Lady of the Grapes – set on the prime Covent Garden thoroughfare of Maiden Lane – would be a wine-sloshing shoe-in anyway. But the bar's MO transcends aesthetics: here, there's an overarching focus on female wine-makers. Owner-sommelier Carole Bryan has collated a list of around 350 bottles, an impressively hefty number given such a traditionally parochial industry. Head to their International Women's Day tastings to 'throw bottles of delicious wine in the face of the patriarchy!'. Sisters really *are* doing it for themselves.

16 Maiden Lane, WC2E 7NJ
Nearest station: Covent Garden
ladyofthegrapes.com

7

WINEMAKERS CLUB

Under-arch gem with a vinous legacy

Behind an oversized wooden door beneath the Holborn Viaduct, the twinkling rooms now home to the Winemakers Club have heritage: there's been a wine merchant at this site for almost 80 years, a lineage that includes one of the first Oddbins stores. John Baum opened this simple and atmospheric bar in 2014, as an offshoot to the family importers. Back then, they were mostly repping Tuscan wine region Montalcino, but the bar's popularity demanded a wider scope, and they now list a mix of bottles, from hefty German and Burgundy wines to snazzier fringe stuff.

41a Farringdon Street, EC4A 4AN
Nearest station: Farringdon
thewinemakersclub.co.uk

8

UNCORKED

City-based merchants of prestige

Tucked down a side street near Finsbury Circus, Uncorked is perhaps the textbook City vintners. Which is to say, it's abundant with classic bordeaux, burgundies and champagnes, there's a heady provision of account-emptying, top-end bottles and it's had past critical nods from old-school viticulture rags like *Decanter* (still, along with Jancis Robinson's musings in the *Financial Times*, the last word in trad wine journalism). Looking to invest? They also take en primeur orders (meaning you buy the wine before it's been bottled, typically receiving it a few years after vintage) and offer storage services in bonded warehouses for customers without the space or inclination to cellar their own party juice.

22 Copthall Avenue, EC2R 7DN
Nearest station: Moorgate
uncorked.co.uk

9

ST. JOHN

Ace own-label bottles at a meaty marvel

Three decades in, Fergus Henderson and Trevor Gulliver's monochromatic Smithfield mainstay is as synonymous with wine as it is the nose-to-tail ethos on which it made its name. Few epicurean experiences are as blissful as settling into the clattery bar for a plate of devilled kidneys and a bottle of St. JOHN-label claret, beaujolais or, if the sun's out, a beaming, champagne-style crémant. They work 100 per cent directly with producers, and have done since the off, a logistically masochistic undertaking involving 'knocking on doors in the twilight, somewhere in the profonde...' says Gulliver. They also run their own winery, Boulevard Napoléon, in the medieval village of La Livinière in Minervois, southern France.

26 St John Street, EC1M 4AY
Nearest station: Farringdon
stjohnrestaurant.com

10
LE CORDON BLEU

Oenophile masterclasses in Bloomsbury

Bloomsbury's Cordon Bleu cookery school – spun-off the totemic Parisian original and, crucially, inventor of coronation chicken in 1953 – runs some of the capital's most esteemed wine courses for budding oenophiles and experts alike. There's simple wine tastings and four-week 'Initiation to Wine Appreciation' courses, pairing masterclasses (with cheese, canapés or summer foods, say), Old vs New World deep-dives and hospitality-focused sessions on wine in restaurants. And for future sommeliers and wine world professionals, full-bore diplomas: a comprehensive immersion taking in everything from sensory analysis and production to the minutiae of customer service and glassware. There's something here for everyone.

15 Bloomsbury Square, WC1A 2LS
Nearest station: Holborn
cordonbleu.edu

11

QUALITY WINES

Boozy Chop House offshoot with a cult chef

Such is the ardour directed at the casually divine dishes (god-tier gildas; pimenton and pork bifana rolls; shattering pig fat cannoli filled with Pump Street chocolate...) knocked out by chef Nick Bramham at this gothically candlelit sister site to Farringdon's Quality Chop House, that it's sometimes easy to overlook the wet stuff. But maintain focus: the stuffed cellar is a truly bounteous thing, with a heady cache of riesling and chenin blanc amid the wider, overwhelmingly Old World inventory (which also includes several cracking vintages, exalted champagnes and large-format bottles for the deep pocketed – or extra thirsty).

88 Farringdon Road, EC1R 3EA
Nearest station: Farringdon
qualitywinesfarringdon.com

12

THE 10 CASES

Ever-changing bottles near Neal Street

The clue's in the name at this sweetly rattly, bedded-in bistro off Seven Dials. There are around 25 wines on the menu: ten reds, ten whites, a few pinks, oranges and sparkling, each bought in caches of ten cases (so, 120 bottles each), and after they're drunk, they're gone. It's an approachable way of sloshing back interesting wines – glasses range from £6.50 to £10 – and the permuting selection skews across the spectrum, from light beaujolais and heftier clarets to dark rosés and glou glou oranges, so there's always something to suit the food (and London's calamitously change-able weather). Dusty chalkboards, Thonet-style bistro chairs and humming ceiling fans complete the scene.

16 Endell Street, WC2H 9BB
Nearest station: Covent Garden
10cases.co.uk

13

HALF CUT MARKET

Lockdown merchant turned destination restaurant

Located on the York Way Riviera (i.e. the no-man's land between Kentish Town and Caledonian Road), Half Cut Market is a Covid-era bottle shop turned wine-focused eatery, with a brilliant list courtesy of co-founder Holly Willcocks (who also finds the time to head up the wine programme at Tomos Parry's lauded Mountain in Soho). Low-intervention dominates – albeit erring away from the more bonkers and farmier end of the spectrum – and by-the-glass pours come from the keg. Zig Zag, a col fondo-method 'prosecco' from Dorset's Langham, and a gluggable red from Les Vans de Pirouettes collective in Alsace are evergreen; fine foils to scallop crudo with espelette, or a burnished pork schnitzel with brown butter.

396 York Way, N7 9LW
Nearest station: Caledonian Road
halfcut.world

14

THE DRAPERS ARMS

Quintessential pub with an overachieving list

A duck-egg-blue pile on a Barnsbury back street, the Drapers is a perennial 'best pub' shoe-in for London's clued-up gastronauts. The appeal is threefold. There's the merrily Old World, high-ceilinged, cod-Georgian aesthetic. The city's best suet crust pies and other robustly satisfying modern European eats. And owner Nick Gibson's stonking great cellar, which has earned a coveted Star Wine List entry for its heavily curated, largely trad-European focus (give or take some new-school South African bottles and minor curveballs, like a Tenerife white laced with Pedro Ximénez, a grape more associated with sweet, sticky sherry). It starts cheap but the markups are egalitarian, so there are wild bargains to be found at the top end, too.

44 Barnsbury Street, N1 1ER
Nearest station: Highbury & Islington
thedrapersarms.com

15

HECTOR'S

Garrulous local gem with a banging back room

Jolly neighbourhood vibes are rife at this De Beauvoir gem, known by its yellow awning, antiquated 'J. Scott & Sons' signage of the shop's former occupier and throngs of merry sloshers spilling onto the pavement. It's equally Mediterranean inside: all cerulean tiles, a teeny blackboard of charcuterie, cheese and tinned fish and shelves straining with natural varietals from smaller domaines (and particularly cooler clime French wines, as well as those from Italy, Spain, Greece, Portugal and Georgia). Anyone seeking something older should head past the bar to the backroom, laden with cult bottles and rare finds, many laid down when the bar opened in 2021.

49a Ardleigh Road, N1 4HS
Nearest station: Dalston Junction
hectorslondon.co.uk

16

CADET

Perfect pours and serious meats

Three's a crowd but four is a party. Such is the case with Cadet: founded by wine importers Tom Beattie and Francis Roberts, chef Jamie Smart and charcuterie maker George Jephson. The bar is blissful: a vision of muted formica, salvaged enamel lampshades and nifty posters specially designed for the bar's winemaker events. Drinks are top-tier, factoring everything from sunny, sparkling pinot gris (a peachier proxy of pinot grigio, but grown outside of Italy) courtesy of Austrian winemaker Christophe Lindenlaub, to fervently sustainable blended reds from Belgium's Wijngaard Lijsternest. The food is equally killer; Jephson's painterly pâté en croute truly one for the ages.

57 Newington Green, N16 9PX
Nearest station: Canonbury
cadetlondon.com

17

DAN'S

Democratic delineations in scruffbag surrounds

Redolent of your bohemian grandmother's front room – replete with scuffed furnishings and trailing succulents – and laden with fridges scrawled with directives like 'SUPER HECTIC SKINSY', 'YUMMY CHARDY' and 'BANGERS UNDER £20', it's fair to say that Dan's takes a casual approach to the cliquish world of wine. Opened in 2021 as an offshoot to importers Natty Boy Wines (now Parched), there's no particular geographic remit (though the macerated whites by Alsatian producer Vincent Gross get a good showing) – just a focus on 'properly made wines from conscientious growers', explains the eponymous Dan Long. The by-the-glass list is egalitarian, too: no hifalutin mention of grapes, regions or growers, just options of Fizz, Crisp White, Easy Skinsy or Turbo Chilled Red.

2–4 Tottenham Road, N1 4BZ
Nearest station: Dalston Junction
dans.wine

18

THE CELLARS

Great drinks and deli goods

Crouch End's eminent bar–shop–deli began as a gentle railing against big business, when Oddbins man Andrea Coaro decided it was time to fill shelves of his own. Back in 2017 this meant small producers, but now the offering is mostly natural, skewing a tad to the cleaner (i.e. not so funky) side. Surfaces are festooned with supplementary cheese, charcuterie and, er, cigars, and there's a dinky backroom and garden in which to sup, eat and smoke them. Chuck in monthly tastings and ad hoc shindigs – the holy trinity of a 'mortadella, focaccia and lambrusco' party, for instance – and you've a beloved local jewel.

55 The Broadway, N8 8DT
Nearest stations: Hornsey, Crouch Hill
thecrouchendcellars.com

19

TRULLO WINE BAR

Italian classic's pint-sized sibling

It's as it sounds: an adjoining sister bar to Canonbury's evergreen Italian restaurant, where the wine is low-intervention-focused but not challengingly so, championing sustainable growers and wineries creating expressive – but, they stress, 'stable' – wines (which is to say, nothing to freak out the uninitiated). Pan-European varietals are drawn from importers like Modal and Les Caves de Pyrene, as well as listings from folks like Penzer wines' Joe Haynes (who also heads up the offering at Cloth, no.3). The space is a Lilliputian vision of deep-blue velvet and spare seating designed by Day Studio, who also did the restaurant proper back in 2010; the snacks list heavy on Italian salumi and oil-slicked focaccia.

300–302 St Paul's Road, N1 2LH
Nearest station: Highbury & Islington
trullorestaurant.com

20
SHRINE TO THE VINE

Colourful wine mag's spin-off shop

Noble Rot's spin-off retail enterprise has two locations: one opposite the original Rotter bastion on Lamb's Conduit Street (no.1), another on the anxious sighthound and gorpcore highway of Broadway Market. Both are fairly minimalist, with knowledgeable staff and a laconic chillwave soundtrack to cushion the inevitable spend. The remit is the same as the restaurant – wines that the owners enjoy drinking, whether pocket-money price txakoli (a lower-alcohol sparkling wine common in the Basque region) or more wallet-dusting options like hefty vintages of German rieslings and French burgundies. Oh, and the shop's whizzy logo is by Jose Mendez, who also drew the near-iconic Chin Chin label and a raft of their magazine covers. All hail.

27 Broadway Market, E8 4PH
Nearest station: London Fields
Other location: Bloomsbury
shrinetothevine.co.uk

21
107

Second coming of a scene-defining pioneer

The sudden demise of P. Franco – perhaps *the* formative second-wave London natural wine bar – in March 2023 was a seismic shock to the city's wine buffs. But from the ashes rose 107: P. Franco v.2 in all but name, helmed by the same manager, William Gee, in the same spot, with the same mission. It's a little more fanatical than most. Gee is almost radically committed to the natural cause, growing grapes 'in an environment that encourages life' (i.e. always fermented with wild yeasts, with trace amounts of stabilising sulphur), but it remains breezily informal: no bookings, a single communal table, weird and wonderful bottles with minimal markups and feted guest chefs working over a couple of hot plates.

107 Lower Clapton Road, E5 0NP
Nearest station: Hackney Central
107wine.co.uk

BAR MENU

Bread + butter 3.5
Olives 4
Crisps + guindillas 7
Sobrassed + honey 9
Cured pork belly 9 or Salami 7
Mozzarella + Artichoke 13
Mussells escabeche 12
Beef tartare + Pane carasau 14
Cantabrian anchovies 19
Cheese + quince 15
Green Salad 6
Chocolate ganache 8

FRANK'S
(DUBLIN)
107
1982O
NOVEMBER

22

FOREST WINES

E17's exemplar bottle shop

Bottle shops are ten-a-penny in this town, but Walthamstow's sylvan stalwart – now a decade in – is a Platonic ideal of the form. In 2014, the natural wine boom was still in its infancy, but owner Jana Postulkova and her husband Ali's hand-picked inventory filled a nascent niche in their corner of northeast London. And it still does: the duo collaborate with over 20 different suppliers, building especially strong connections with producers like Slobodne in Slovakia (of which they stock a zero-alcohol grüner for the temperate) and Staffelter Hof in the German Mosel (creator of the inimitably named Little Bastard riesling, with grapes grown on an estate bought from Napoleon's government in 1805). A neon exterior mural completes the scene.

149 Forest Road, E17 6HE
Nearest station: Blackhorse Road
forestwines.com

23
WINGNUT

Fascinating finds in a market shack shop

What started life as a stall in Netil Market (an epicurean enclave at the foot of London Fields) is now a fully fledged shack. After cutting his teeth in Spain, where he was particularly taken with Madrid's bar culture ('Intimate, and hot, where strangers met strangers'), founder Charlie Carr was deeply uninspired by what he saw as 'static' London wine lists, homogeneously marked by the same producers and bottles. He founded Wingnut to counter this, seeking out new wines by young, underrepresented makers, and buying in super-small quantities (usually two or three bottles of each cuvée). It's a philosophy repped in the shack's Thirsty Thursday tastings, and via the list at Papi – the wonderfully outré bistro he runs with chef Matthew Scott nearby.

Netil Market, 13–23 Westgate Street, E8 3RU
Nearest station: London Fields
wingnutwines.com

24

PLANQUE

Design-savvy drinkers' clubhouse

Born in 2021 of founder Jonathan Alphandery's decade-long foray into wine collecting – the spoils of which had gotten so out of hand that he was compelled to create a space in which to share it – Planque is a hyper-chic, 60-cover restaurant, bar and member's club, where one can cellar their own bottle hoards. It occupies a truly whizz-bang space under the Haggerston railway arches, replete with a YSL-blue cubbyhole, a glass-fronted cellar for eyeballing the elusive and rarefied bottles therein, minimalist strip lights and HAY 'Rey' dining chairs, industrial venting and pastel-painted girders, all conceived by Copenhagen's Studio X. Seeking a cool place to store your verticals? This is it.

322–324 Acton Mews, E8 4EA
Nearest station: Haggerston
planque.co.uk

25

JOYAU

Cerulean-tinted arch bar

A faultless example of a community-focused wine bar, Joyau – French for 'jewel' – is a blissfully simple, blue-and-white bolthole in a corrugated arch space, and (along with the buzzy Wanstead Tap directly next door) the nucleus of Winchelsea Road's cheerful scene. Founded by an ex-Noble Rot (no.1) staffer and inspired by beloved Parisian bars like the 11th's La Buvette, the offering is non-dogmatic but features natural-leaning bottles with a French focus, simply constructed small plates and occasional chef residencies. It's a shiny example of the form and a perfect meeting point for the hip young parents of Forest Gate.

353 Winchelsea Road, E7 0AQ
Nearest station: Wanstead Park
joyau.co

26

BRAWN

Elder statesman on Columbia Road

Brawn is a bona fide old hand in the natural wine scene. A light-filled corner restaurant recalling nothing as much as a Provençal classroom from the 1950s, it's reverently muttered about for both Ed Wilson's Italianate cooking and a nuanced wine offering. Among others, they've an intimate relationship with importers Les Caves de Pyrene – affording access to the deeper, more esteemed recesses of their inventory. Examples of such treats include vintages from Yvon Métras, one of Beaujolais' 'Gang of Four' – a group of 1980s vigernons who revolutionised low-intervention winemaking in the region. Cheaper pours might include Jean Maupertuis' lightly funky gamay (a fresh, light red) or something from ace Catalonian winemaker Partida Creus (with its iconic minimalist bottle designs).

49 Columbia Road, E2 7RG
Nearest station: Hoxton
brawn.co

27
SUNE

Wild libations from a wine-world heroine

Statuesque sommelier, author and general wine-world doyenne Honey Spencer revitalised the small plates and natural wine model with this, a beatific Broadway Market-ish spot opened with ex-Noma general manager Charlie Sims. The list ditches cult and status wines, erring instead towards those that 'are alive and present a multi-dimensional experience, especially when paired with food'. Obtusely poetic, sure, but fascinating in practice, whether Lebanese bottles created with ancient indigenous grapes like marini or dhaw al-qamar, and the occasional insanely wild (and pricey) Japanese varietal. The rest of the concept (down to the pastel paint-flecked menu) is equally honed; even the abstemious should visit for the croque monsieur topped with raw beef.

129a Pritchard's Road, E2 9AP
Nearest station: London Fields
sune.restaurant

28
SAGER + WILDE

Timeless idol on the Hackney Road

Michael Sager's Hackney Road old-hand is a natural wine second-waver still kicking it with the best of the upstarts. The lists don't err too funky – 'It's the Icarus metaphor,' he says. 'You want to fly close to the sun, but you don't want to get burned' (as in, where palatably odd becomes a bit too 'farmyard') – but there are happy concessions to the public's unstoppable thirst for chilled red and orange wines. Sager is well on the zeitgeist when ascendant and unusual regions are going gangbusters (new-wave California and Oregon, or Hungarian wines, say). Chuck in some monochromatically moody interiors – with a bar constructed from old glass pavement tiles, and some warm globe lighting – and the seminal scene is complete.

193 Hackney Road, E2 8JL
Nearest station: Hoxton
sagerandwilde.com

29

ORANJ

Industrial chic and borderless pours

Yes, finding this hip natty wine pit can feel like a challenge – it's located in a barely reconstructed stable-cum-warehouse space behind a nondescript backstreet door – but it's worth persevering. The by-the-glass list offers a thrilling traipse around both well-trodden and unheralded regions (from omnipresent Lazio label Le Coste and its gossamer-white Bianchetto blend, to the cherry-red Dark Horse sparkling from Petr Korab in Czech Moravia). The kitchen sees a revolving host of pop-ups, many from overseas, such as Coko Becker's Mexican-inspired, boundary-pushing cuisine. Questionable warehouse acoustics, but less yapping = more sipping.

14 Bacon Street, E1 6LF
Nearest station: Shoreditch High Street
oranj.co.uk

30

IDLE MOMENTS

Japanese records and natty bottles

Less a venn diagram than a perfect circle, an appreciation for luridly labelled natural wine, archival jazz and teeny, tiny hats is now inextricably synonymous with the urbane hipster of a certain age (i.e. wretched late thirties). Idle Moments – a Columbia Road record, audio equipment and bottle shop, spun-off from Dalston's Japanese restaurant Brilliant Corners – capitalises on all three, with a curation of low-intervention bottles and a bevy of fine wax sourced by the Tokyo-based dealer Vinyl Delivery Service. Perfect for when you can't possibly countenance returning home without a bottle of biodynamic frizzante and a copy of Coltrane's *Giant Steps* in your tote.

86 Columbia Road, E2 7QB
Nearest station: Hoxton
idle-moments.com

31

RENEGADE

City viniculture on the Blackhorse Beer Mile

E17's preeminent (only) winery, Renegade is the eight-year lovechild of jaded ex-financial services man Warwick Smith. In 2016, the philosophy was simply 'nice wines'. Now, it's more like a craft brewery for wine, eschewing the rigid parameters that established regions, family traditions and appellation guidelines demand to create something truly original: whether sauvignon made in England with French grapes and Kiwi yeast, or a hopped English sparkling that's an IPA on the nose, tropical fizz on the palate (dubbed Bethnal Bubbles). Singular, too, are the labels – each displaying the peepers of a regular joe. Anyone can apply, and repeat vintages use the same model each year, their eyes ageing with the cuvée.

7 Lockwood Way, E17 5RB
Nearest station: Blackhorse Road
renegadelondonwine.com

32
TOP CUVÉE

Vividly hued basement boozing

The capital's wine scene may be fertile, but many new-school spots do err somewhat samey in their muted aesthetics. Not so of Top Cuvée, with its logo designed by maximalist cartoon artist Turbo Island, and an eye-popping house palette of orange and black. The name itself is an irreverent nose-thumbing to wine-world snobbery, with everyday drinkers often denied the 'top cuvées' by snooty Michelin sommeliers. Their Bethnal Green basement bar, bottle shop and gourmet hotdog emporia is a doozy. A dribble of beer and champagne aside, they import 99 per cent of their inventory themselves, and they run a vino masterclass on site every other Wednesday. Nifty merch, too.

250a Bethnal Green Road, E2 0AA
Nearest station: Bethnal Green
Other location: Highbury
topcuvee.com

33

GNARLY VINES

Established bottle shop with cool house collabs

A sister hustle to their Clapton Craft beer stores, industry veterans William Jack and Tom McKim's Walthamstow emporia has been a hotbed for east London oenophiles since 2017. They originally sought to quash the apprehension around organic, biodynamic and low-intervention wines. Now folks are more au fait with appellations, the USP is more the provision of hard-to-source allocations (smatterings of new wave Burgundy or super-low-production Jura wines, say) and exclusive Gnarly Vines-labelled collabs, like a dry-farmed xarel·lo produced by Penedès's Celler Cal Costas, and two garnachas (grenache) from Vinicola Reverte in Navarra (the vivid labels of which are almost as vivacious as the plonk itself).

464 Hoe Street, E17 9AH
Nearest station: Leyton Midland Road
gnarlyvines.co.uk

34

NEWCOMER WINES

Austrian wines and a secret garden

Yet *another* top-tier drinking den on the Dalston–
De Beauvoir vino axis, Newcomer keeps a keen
focus on wines from Austria and unusual, esoteric
grapes from more leftfield locales (e.g. Babić and
Pošip from Croatia, or Rèze from Switzerland),
the collective of which they've snappily deemed
the 'New Old World'. Beginning life as a Box-
park unit in 2014 before morphing into a roomier
bar–bottle shop, the hidden suntrap garden is one
of the sweetest places in town to get acquainted
with an ice-cold bottle of superlative blaufränk-
isch pét-nat (the dark-skinned grape has vaguely
peppery notes) from Markus Altenburger, a keen
biodynamicist and shop fave maker who's been
with them since the start.

5 Dalston Lane, E8 3DF
Nearest station: Dalston Junction
newcomerwines.com

35

BRAT

Fab vintages and flame-licked food

Welsh chef Tomos Parry's rustic paean to the flame-licked cookery of Spain's Basque region has summited many a London food list since opening in 2018. Gannets may be taken with the charred turbot and smoked potatoes, but the wine selection is a thing of elegance, too. Despite the food's remit, it's heavy on the Gallic stuff and there's also eye on zippy Greek reds and a good trudge around the Iberian peninsula – particularly in the trough-loads of nutty, amber-coloured amontillado and oxidative sherries from Jerez to round out your meal. Special dispensation, too, is given to the complex works of Burgundian winemaker Dominique Lucas's Les Vignes de Paradis label, fashioned on the hills above Lake Geneva.

4 Redchurch Street, E1 6JL
Nearest station: Shoreditch High Street
bratrestaurant.co.uk

36

POLENTINA

Regional Italian gem in a factory canteen

'Converted textile mill canteen on a dingy industrial estate in Bow' doesn't exactly scream cosmopolitan must-visit. But Polentina – a rustic Italian diner with views through a glass wall onto the workshop floor of a sustainable apparel company – is one-of-a-kind. Chef–founder Sophia Massarella's comforting, homestyle cooking draws on her central Italian and east Austrian heritage, and beyond. Sommelier Giulia Dowgier's nuanced list starts in northern Italy (give or take some bottles from further afield) and works its way down the boot, taking in citrussy, saline Ligurain whites, peachy Trebbiano oranges from Tuscany and electrically tinted rosé from Umbria along the way. Chow: bella.

1 Bowood House, Empson Street, E3 3LT
Nearest stations: Bromley-by-Bow, Devons Road
polentina.com

37

FORZA WINE

Glou glou pours with pristine panoramas

There are few seasonal SE London experiences as definitive as schlepping to the top floor of Peckham Rye's station-adjacent Market building, settling into a glass (or four) of crisp pét-nat and a few Italian-ish titbits and gawping, slack-jawed and awestruck, at a salmon-pink sunset creeping over the city skyline. But such is the case with Forza Wine's lofty setting. Stunner aspect aside, it's a fantastic bar – with a short 'n' sweet list of hip pan-European bottles, including some newer-fangled house wines. They've a second site on the National Theatre's third floor terrace if you prefer Brutalist Bankside splendour to Peckham grit.

The Rooftop, 133a Rye Lane, SE15 4BQ
Nearest station: Peckham Rye
Other location: Bankside
forzawine.com

38

ELLIOT'S

Buzzy market go-to with sensational snacks

A Borough Market stalwart since 2011, Elliot's has long carried a torch for low-intervention wines created with the planet in mind. The restaurant is – a là thrumming bustle of Stoney Street outside – fast-paced, buzzy and cosmopolitan, reflected in a frequently changing list of natural gems. Around a tenth is made up of lightly quaffable, seasonal juice; the rest a deep dive into creative wine-making and pure expression of terroir (ebulliently fresh bottles from Laura Brennan Bissel's Californian label, Inconnu, say; or sparkling gems from Limeburn Hill, in the Chew Valley near Bristol). The kitchen's Isle of Mull cheese puffs and wild garlic calzones are exceptional, too.

12 Stoney Street, SE1 9AD
Nearest station: London Bridge
elliots.london

39
CHEZ BRUCE

Common-side classic with an ocean-deep cellar

Wandsworth Common's totemic neighbourhood restaurant – presided over by the titular Bruce Poole since 1995 – is as feted for its 900-ish bottle cellar as it is the timeless array of classic French and Mediterranean dishes. The trad top-end is well represented (and often below market-standard markups), with a big focus on France, a good provision of Tuscan wine, a smattering of South African and new-school Eastern European (plus a few natural wines from the cleaner end of the spectrum; 'I don't discriminate!' says head sommelier Matilda Di Cecio). It's all quaffed in a white-clothed, overlit space that's only more enjoyable for the throwback vibes. A tied-on classic (that your parents will love).

2 Bellevue Road, SW17 7EG
Nearest station: Wandsworth Common
chezbruce.co.uk

40

TÓU

Summery wines and superlative sandos

Asceticism is everything at TÓU, a quirky first-floor spot in Borough Market that focuses on two things: Japanese-style katsu sandos and pét-nat wine. The pairing is genius: the effervescent, lower-ABV, fruity, funky pep of the wine (reds, whites and rosés) a perfect foil to the elevated, junky umami of the sandwiches. Elsewhere, there's a lean selection of pickles, a slider, some croquettes and a coffee–biscoff sundae as delicious as it is weird-looking – plus a bevy of 'regular' wines for the fizz-averse.

Upstairs at the Globe Tavern,
8 Bedale Street, SE1 9AL
Nearest station: London Bridge
tou-london.com

41

BAR LEVAN

Paris-style Peckham cave with killer tunes

This urbane dedication to the dinky wine dens of Paris might be eternally cool Peckham's hippest spot. The list is dynamic: a constant rotation of producers and a juxtaposition of styles, from cleanly approachable to ferociously funky. House wines are served from the keg and include white and orange from Italy, red from Spain and rosé from France, while the cellar selection spans cult makers, bottles with age and a few sought after unicorns. A monthly tasting event – 'Strictly Bangers' – is self-consciously un-nerdy and wilfully raucous, not least for the 'open decks' musical policy. 'No death metal!' they plead.

Unit 5, 12–16 Blenheim Grove, SE15 4QL
Nearest station: Peckham Rye
barlevan.co.uk

42

DYNAMIC VINES

Biodynamic warehouse with killer tastings

Strung through a few rail-rattled arches on a dowdy business estate, Dynamic Vines are the country's biggest biodynamic importers. They mostly work trade, but are open to the public each Friday and Saturday for ad hoc tastings and in-person shopping. Greater still are the Annual Portfolio Tasting days, where you can borrow a glass and stumble your way around the site, tasting wines by scores of visiting vignerons (including the folks behind esteemed labels like Radikon, an orange wine titan on the Slovenian-Italian border, and Emidio Pepe, one of Italian Abruzzo's most feted makers). It's an enlightening event and, if you choose to swallow rather than spit, an absolutely soaked endurance test.

Unit 5, Discovery Business Park,
St James's Road, SE16 4RA
Nearest station: Bermondsey
dynamicvines.com

43

BOROUGH WINES

Market-based tap-wine purveyors

Wine on tap isn't a wholly unremarkable phenomenon in London 2024, but don't underestimate how outré reusable bottles and plonk gushing from the keg would have been back in 2002, when Borough Wines was born. A semi-alfresco shop on the chaotic market's southern side, championing small-scale and sustainable vignerons (what else?), there are myriad European bottles to buy in addition to the affordably priced house wines on tap. Come the summer, there are some token fruitier offerings (including Aperol slushies) and frequent tastings of recently arrived varietals. Hot tip: beforehand, offset the booze with a superlative sausage roll from the Ginger Pig opposite.

Borough Market, SE1 1TL
Nearest station: London Bridge
instagram.com/boroughwines

44

BAR DASKAL

Iberian grapes at a tapas titan offshoot

The marble-clad, tapas-hawking restaurant group Barrafina has long been shorthand for some of the most sophisticated Spanish bites in London – so it was only a matter of time until the guys behind it expanded their focus to the stronger stuff. Enter Bar Daskal, named after the owners' grandfather, Vladimir Daskaloff: a Bulgarian emigré who settled in Mallorca and made a name as a Balearic artist (echoed in the warm, tactile interiors – a reference to both Vlad's studio and the family pad in Estellencs). Even chicer than the heritage is the list: a short, sweet smorgasbord of top-drawer Spanish wines, vermuts and sherries – perfect for washing back oozing wedges of tortilla while dreaming of the Med.

16 Park Street, SE1 9AB
Nearest station: London Bridge
bardaskal.co.uk

45

LULU'S

Fringe Euro varietals in serene south London

A cosmopolitan bolthole – awash with flecked marble and soaped wood – on the buzzy drag outside Herne Hill station, Lulu's vaguely embraces the Parisian *cave à manger* model (that is, a cultivated wine store with a supporting menu of banging dishes). The wine list focuses on lesser-trodden regions, with a 'disproportionately large' amount of high-acidity white and fruitier red Polish varietals from Leeds' Central Wines, plus bits and pieces from Georgia, Moldova, Slovenia and fringe French regions (among the Old World standards). They hold occasional tastings of these, and all the booze is bolstered by an array of zesty seasonal plates and pretty inventory of bijous tinned fish and other store cupboard staples.

291 Railton Road, SE24 0JP
Nearest station: Herne Hill
lulus.london

46

MOTHER SUPERIOR

Plague-era gem gone local go-to

A COVID side hustle – which kicked off selling magnums of biodynamic Beaujolais Nouveau through a socially distanced open window – turned go-to neighbourhood vintners, Mother Superior's broad aim is to bring natural wines of provenance and quality to the Nunhead community (with the added visual boon of their saintly nun logo and dashing, beige-pink frontage). The stock is fab: thrilling seasonal classics for the 'heads, but with plenty under £20, and they highlight female producers, super-sustainable and homegrown wines as a point of practice. Desperate to get a taste now, *now, NOW*? Hit the shop's basement bar or street-side benches and pop a cork or cap.

26 Nunhead Green, SE15 3QF
Nearest station: Nunhead
mothersuperior.co.uk

47

SALTHOUSE BOTTLES

Airy Brockley bottle shop

Launched in 2016 as a craft beer store with some supplementary wines, Salthouse has since changed tack and gone full vino, carving out a niche as one of southeast London's best emporia of low-intervention labels (some particularly zingy British bottles from south London importer Wines Under the Bonnet among them). It's very much a locals' spot, inclusive and garrulous (much like Joyce, the breezy, casual bar up the road that the founders also run), with an ever-morphing list reflecting the most interesting seasonal bottles arriving in-shop. Not sated? They also run Brockley Natural Wine Club, a charming, intermittent tasting event held at the bar.

12 Coulgate Street, SE4 2RW
Nearest station: Brockley
salthousebottles.com

48

CANTON ARMS

Bustling gastro-boozer with great taps

Bedfellow of the brilliant Anchor & Hope and the Clarence Tavern (in Waterloo and Stoke Newington, respectively), Stockwell's Canton Arms was once an infamously salty boozer, before being transformed into south London's finest gastropub in 2010. A level of winsome grit remains (mostly in the loos) and the aesthetic is pleasingly unpolished (deep red walls, shelves of pickle, chutney and fermenting jars, hand-scrawled blackboards). The homely grub is perfectly offset by a pan-European wine list of surprising heft. Gallic names reign supreme, but there's a sprinkling of biodynamic and organic bottles (including an orange from Italian makers Radikon, a true pub boon) and there are various ripper tap wines available by carafe, bottle or magnum. Settle in.

177 South Lambeth Road, SW8 1XP
Nearest station: Stockwell
cantonarms.com

49

VERAISON

Low-key atmosphere on the SE5 strip

'Unprepossessing' might be the best word to describe this beloved den, sat stumbling distance from gastropub the Camberwell Arms (also a blinder for wine) and demarcated by the neon-purple beacon of a grape sign in the window. The simplicity is the appeal, though. Here, you'll find a heaving wall of shelves full of natural bottles to drink in or take home, a counter-top chiller full of charcuterie, pâtés and cheeses to nibble on, some scuffed bistro furnishings and that's about it. But the low-key clout is indisputable: not least as founder Patrycja Lorek formerly worked at the 10 Cases (no.12) and is hitched to John Baum, head honcho of the Winemakers Club (no.7) in Farringdon.

78 Camberwell Church Street, SE5 8QZ
Nearest station: Denmark Hill
veraisonwines.co.uk

50

40 MALTBY STREET

Maltby Street Market's second-wave titan

Public face of fab importers Gergovie (pronounced 'ZHER-zho-VEE', named after the Auvergne plateau in from which it first sourced its wines) and second-wave icon open since 2011, 40 Maltby has become a place of pilgrimage for plonk fiends. Rightly so. Their repurposed railway arch home is perpetually thrumming; the seasonal small dishes dreamy; and the colourful metal shelves laden with an all-natural stock of takeaway bottles that can be drunk in with a £20 corkage. The initial regional ambit has expanded a tad, though they cite natural wine legends Patrick Bouju and Justine Loiseau's Domaine la Bohème (a label stocked since the bar opened) as a winery they still particularly chime with. No bookings, but entirely worth the wait.

40 Maltby Street, SE1 3PG
Nearest station: London Bridge
40maltbystreet.com

51

BLACKBOOK WINERY

Dual-varietal bottles near Battersea Park

After years of travelling around Europe working on sustainable vineyards, Sergio Verrillo was inspired to start urban winery Blackbook in 2017 with his wife Lyndsey. Their microproduction of around 3,500 bottles a year largely uses grapes sourced from south Essex (and other locales no more than two hours away). Single varietal chardonnay and pinot noir wines form the core range, but they also knock up an experimental range of weirder ad hoc blends. It's all produced in a 100-year-old Victorian archway where they run weekly tours and tastings. In a cute nod to their wider surroundings, the bottle labels are designed with abstract references to things like tiles at the Tate Britain (the Painter of Light chardonnay) or native wildlife (in the Nightjar pinot).

Arch 41, London Stone Business Estate,
Broughton Street, SW8 3QR
Nearest station: Queenstown Road
blackbookwinery.com

52

SOIF

Parisian ambiance on Battersea Rise

The late Terroirs may have helped lay the foundations for Paris-style natty libations in London – but its spirit lives on in Soif: a charming bistro–bar just off Clapham Common, started as a spin-off to the Charing Cross icon. The name translates variously as 'thirst' and 'lust'. Such are the desires prompted by a glance at the estimably lengthy *carte* of biodynamic and low-intervention bottles, many made by winemakers employing labour-intensive production methods (like using horses rather than tractors) and cherry-picking things from ancillary and upcoming zones like Greece, Slovenia, Oregon and er, Welsh Monmouthshire (namely, Ancre Hill's fabulous pét-nat and chardonnay). Factor in monthly precision-focus on different countries, and you've a package *complète*.

27 Battersea Rise, SW11 1HG
Nearest station: Clapham Junction
soif.co

53

LONDON CRU

The inner city's OG makers

Stumbling distance from the austere avenues of Brompton Cemetery, with an approach demarked by a snazzy grape mural, is London's original city winemakers. Its line of small-batch vintages takes in smashable pét-nat, citrussy blanc de blanc (a type of champagne made only with white grapes) and rosé fizz, as well as pinot noir and chardonnay. They now harvest their grapes for bottles forthcoming at Foxhole – a West Sussex vineyard bought in 2023, laden with pinot noir, pinot gris and bacchus. As well as conventional tours, you can also embrace your inner vigneron with a five-hour 'winemaker for a day' ticket – delving into grape structure, harvest logistics, classic styles and some DIY blending to create a (potentially appalling) personal cuvée to neck on the tube home.

21–27 Seagrave Road, SW6 1RP
Nearest station: West Brompton
londoncru.co.uk

54

THE PELICAN

First-gen vignerons and dashing digs

How much one enjoys this hyper-chic west London gastro-boozer will be dependant on your tolerance for Arcteryx gilets and gleaming signet rings. But The Pelican is, indubitably, a gem: a vision of distressed, muted palettes, soft lighting and a menu that doesn't so much nod to St. JOHN (no.9) as grapple it to the ground. It also boasts an excellent list brimming with low-intervention gems: from Tim Wildman's Lost in a Field English–Welsh blend pét-nat, to gamay from Beaujolais' Chateau Cambon (made from vines once owned by Jules Chauvet, one of the region's first natural winemakers).

45 All Saints Road, W11 1HE
Nearest station: Westbourne Park
thepelicanw11.com

55

10 GREEK STREET

Soho staple with a great value USP

Low-frills eateries with simple, seasonally led menus and concise lists might be omnipresent these days, but 10 Greek Street has been perfecting this stuff since 2012. It's rightly considered a godfather of the Soho scene, with a canny two-pronged offering. First, a stripped back, 'standard' list of around 15 whites, 15 reds and a few sparklings, plus several sticky sweet and fortified wines, all democratically priced (largely below £60, an anomaly these days). Second, the monthly 'Black Book': a handwritten list of older vintages and rare varietals, one or two bottles of each sold with minimal markups – a miscellanea that utterly deserves the exalted rep. There's also £5 corkage on Fridays if you fancy yourself the expert.

10 Greek Street, W1D 4DH
Nearest station: Tottenham Court Road
10greekstreet.com

56

BAR CRISPIN

Wines grouped by climate in bustling Carnaby

There's a blithely sideways approach to compiling the booze at this kick-ass Kingly Street bar. Rather than country or grape, they've split the list into climate categories, prompting drinkers to think about why wines have a certain profile based on their specific meteorological locale, and grouping bottles under regions defined as Maritime (such as Stellenbosch in South Africa's Western Cape); Continental (Kamptal in Austria); and Mediterranean (such as Roussillon in southern France). They're all bought from producers with penchants for expressing their terroirs and giving back to the land. Not least the Kamptal's Christoph Heiss: a wunderkind vigneron who bottles BC's house grüner (a minerally, slightly acidic and sometimes cloudy white) and cherry-humming 55/45 red-white blend.

19 Kingly Street, W1B 5PY
Nearest station: Oxford Circus
barcrispin.com

57

VINDINISTA

Longstandingly convivial neighbourhood spot

The west London 'hood of Acton is not, alas, over-blessed with brilliant food and drink – apart from Vindinista. The shop's recent inheritor, Canadian Halle Stephens – who also runs boutique wine importer Okanagan Roots and is part of the female importer group CollectEve – has retained the sweet community vibe, but embraced a slightly more leftfield drinks offering. Myriad up-and-coming regions (Moldova, Slovakia, Slovenia, Bulgaria, etc.) abound; there are bargain grab 'n' go standards; and small importers regularly take over the by-the-glass list, with popular sells making their way onto the shelves.

74 Churchfield Rd, W3 6DH
Nearest station: Acton Central
vindinista.com

58

ANDREW EDMUNDS

Swooning Soho stalwart with WSET courses

Palpable was the grief that met the 2022 passing of Andrew Edmunds: art dealer, all-round good egg and long-time proprietor of this eponymous Soho restaurant (often, with its higgledy tables, chiaroscuro lighting and handwritten menus, deemed London's most romantic). Edmunds was a consummate oenophile with a taste for big bordeauxs, burgundies and old German rieslings, and a predilection for modest markups on what he considered thrilling bottles (and somewhat rounded-up ones for those he thought were modish or boring; a de facto tax on un-imaginative pouilly-fumé or sancerre whites). So it remains today, in memory of the man himself. They also run WSET courses and tastings in the private dining room. Chin chin to that.

46 Lexington Street, W1F 0LP
Nearest station: Piccadilly Circus
andrewedmunds.com

59

THE LONDON WINE ACADEMY

Three decades of expertise at various venues

Less historically recherché than the Bleu (no.10) but no less embedded in London wine culture, this transparently titled school operates from a range of venues around town (including Mayfair boozer The Windmill, Brooks Mews Wine House and Bankside's Duke of Sussex gastropub). Detailed intel and introductions to viticulture, regions, history and industry abound, but there's also a focus on more jovial tastings. The Grand Cru Singles events also offer a kind of alternative oenophile dating set-up where one can coquettishly eyeball partners-in-waiting while sloshing back (sorry, *delicately sipping* and expounding on the complexities of) a variety of exquisite bottles.

Various locations
londonwineacademy.com

60
BERRY BROS. & RUDD

Storied chapter in winemaking's history

Jewel of Pall Mall and Britain's oldest wine and spirit merchant (est. 1698), Berry Bros. & Rudd has the lot: two royal warrants, a fascinating history (trivia aplenty, but particularly cataclysmic were the 96 cases of Berry Bros booze lost in the Titanic's sinking), notable patrons (Lord Byron and the Aga Khan among 'em) and, of course, trough after trough of fantastic drink. The credo, explains manager Edwin Dublin, is simple: 'Is it good to drink?' In practice, this means a 5,000-bottle inventory, taking in everything from the shop's uber-reliable Good Ordinary and Extraordinary Clarets through to drops of en primeur and terrifyingly priced vintages.

63 Pall Mall, St James's, SW1Y 5HZ
Nearest station: Green Park
bbr.com

61

WESTWELL

Artistic vineyard below an ancient road

Purveyor of the best labels in the business – artfully abstract takes on the estate's viticulture and agrarian landscapes – Westwell is situated in Kent's North Downs, near the ancient Pilgrim's Way to Canterbury. Run by former music industry bigwig Adrian Pike, it revolves around four key grapes: pinot meunier, pinot noir, chardonnay and ortega, planted across the estate's variously chalky, sandy and flinty soils. The wines, available to sup straight from the tank on an estate tour, are genuinely terrific – especially the saline, tropical white ortega, though the multi-vintage pinot meunier, a lightly burnished blend of grapes from three harvests, gives it a run.

The Vyneyarde, Westwell Lane,
Charing, Kent, TN27 0BW
Nearest station: Charing
westwellwines.com

62

OXNEY

Organic originators and fab fizz

Oxney might be the country's organic scene-leader – not simply for the fact that the vineyard claims to grow a fifth of the UK's organic grapes across its 35 acres, but also because its wines, fashioned with hyper-modern kit in a Grade II-listed oast house (once used to dry hops for beer), are truly ace. Particularly toothsome is the classic sparkling: a blend of grapes suited to the sandy, silty geology, aged on the lees for 36 months (where yeasty sediment is left in the bottle to enrich the flavour), and heady with hints of apple, brioche, honey and other homely stuff. Summer tours take in the fecund vines, while in winter they're a tad more pedagogical and confined to the winery itself.

Hobbs Lane, Rye, East Sussex, TN31 6TU
Nearest station: Rye
oxneyestate.com

63

TILLINGHAM

Regenerative farming and natural wines

If heaven *is* a place on earth, it might just be these 70 arcadian acres near Rye. England's hippest natural vineyard makes for an utterly dreamy getaway, with a bevy of quietly stylish rooms (plus a glamping zone); an enlightening (and blotto) tour and tasting around the site's vines, amphorae pots (traditional ceramic vessels for aging wine) and production warehouse; an outdoor pizza kitchen; and a superb restaurant drawing on the seasonal bounty of Tillingham's regeneratively farmed fields and the surrounding landscape. There's simply nothing like getting half-cut on their new-season 'R' red (all fresh blackberry and violets on the palette) or multi-grape Field Blend wines, ambling the plantation to the estate's viewing platform to breathe in the Sussex idyll.

Dew Farm, Dew Lane, Peasmarsh,
Rye, East Sussex, TN31 6XD
Nearest station: Rye
tillingham.com

64

RATHFINNY

Seaside-ish grower of Britain's best sparkling

East Sussex is a perfect locale for sparkling wine production, its geology very similar to the chalk beds of the Paris Basin and Champagne region (and exactly the reason why various major French winemakers have bought up tracts of the county's land in recent years). It's something known well at Rathfinny: a thwacking great, 600-acre bowl of an estate, which is further blessed with a saline atmosphere from the nearby Channel and a sun-soaked aspect from its South Downs setting. Visiting is a treat: there are two restaurants (one approved by Michelin), a wine bar, tours, a 'dosage tasting' (where one learns how different sugar levels affect a wine), barns and cottages for over-nighting and, yes, gallons of superlative sparkling to spill while you're at it.

Rathfinny Wine Estate, Alfriston,
East Sussex, BN26 5TU
Nearest stations: Seaford
rathfinnyestate.com

65

DURSLADE

Bountiful vines in sunny Somerset

This three-acre vineyard, planted on a clay and limestone slope on the banks of the Brue, near an ancient Roman vine terrace, is run by the folks at Artfarm (a spin-off hospitality company to gallery behemoth Hauser & Wirth). Its 8,000 vines are harvested for bacchus, pinot noir, chardonnay and pinot meunier grapes, then taken to the nearby Bagborough Vineyard and bottled into a concise range of Maid of Bruton wines – all of which can be bought at the cornucopia-style Farm Shop or glugged in the basement bar of its Mayfair outpost.

Durslade Farm, Dropping Lane,
Bruton, Somerset, BA10 0NL
Nearest stations: Bruton
farmshop.co.uk

VINO VERNACULAR

There's no getting around it: the world of wine has long been considered a tad stuffy and impenetrable. A major reason for this is the reams of specialist language reeled off by *oenophiles* (see below) and other wine-world show-offs. We've unpicked some of the potentially confusing terminology below.

Biodynamic: A holistic farming method which embraces astrological planting and pruning (literally doing these things in line with certain moon cycles), biodiversity, polyculture and eschewing chemicals. Seeing the vineyard as a living part of a wider ecosystem, rather than simply a factory for grapes.

Col fondo: A method of making cloudy, fizzy wine where the dead yeasts and sediment (the 'lees') are left in the bottle.

Coravin: A device inserted through a cork with a needle that allows wine to be poured by the glass without oxidising (and can thus stay 'open' for months without spoiling).

Domaine: A vineyard that makes wine from its own grapes.

En primeur: Purchasing wines in advance of being bottled, while they're still in the barrel.

Funky or *farmy*: Common descriptor for natural (a.k.a.

natty) wines laden with divisively punchy flavours and aromas (sometimes like the heady rot of a farmyard).

Glou glou: Typically young, fresh, light-ABV wines that are great for necking in the sun.

Low-intervention and natural wine: A catch-all for organic/biodynamic wines made without the addition of artificial pesticides, yeasts, chemicals, additives and preservatives (give or take a tiny sprinkling of sulphites).

Maceration: Soaking cold, pre-fermented grape juice with the skins, seeds and stalks, to leach tannins and colour (hence the synonymous term *skin contact*). Used to make orange wine (and most reds and rosés).

New World: Typically countries producing wine outside of the Old World regions: Argentina, Australia, South Africa, New Zealand, Chile, Argentina, the US, et al.

Oenophile: A wine enthusiast.

Old World: Typically European and some Mediterranean and Middle Eastern countries (Lebanon, Georgia, et al.) that have a historic culture of winemaking.

Pét-nat: Or *pétillant naturel* – a lightly sparkling wine that's fermented once, a bit, then bottled, the residual sugars continuing the process of fermentation. This is unlike the *Champagne method*, where more yeast and sugar is added to the bottle, prompting a second fermentation (and more fizz).

Tannins: Derived from grape skins, seeds and stems,

tannins make wine taste bitter and dry.

Terroir: The comprehensive natural environment in which wine is produced. Natural wines are sometimes said to express better terroir, because of the lack of additives which might otherwise alter the wine.

Varietal: A single variety of grape as opposed to wine made from a blend of grapes.

Vigneron: Someone who grows grapes for winemaking.

Viniculture: Growing, cultivating and harvesting grapes for winemaking.

Vintage: The year which the grapes used to produce a wine were harvested.

Viticulture: Growing, cultivating and harvesting grapes (but not necessarily for winemaking).

Zero-zero: Natural or low-intervention wine, but with absolutely nothing added in (that is, no stabilising sulphites).

CONTRIBUTORS

Tom Howells is a London-based writer and editor. He's written for *Vogue*, the *Financial Times*, *The Quietus*, *The Fence*, *World of Interiors*, *Wallpaper**, *MacGuffin*, *Time Out* and the *Guardian*, among others. His fave wine is a toss up between Pierre Frick's V Macération pinot gris and Clos Lentiscus's Croac Croac rosado, but he really will neck anything.

Hoxton Mini Press is a small indie publisher based in east London. We make books about London (and beyond) with a dedication to lovely, sustainable production and brilliant photography. When we started the company, people told us 'print was dead'; we wanted to prove them wrong. Books are no longer about information but objects in their own right: things to collect and own and inspire. We are an environmentally conscious publisher, committed to offsetting our carbon footprint. This book, for instance, is 100 per cent carbon compensated, with offset purchased from Stand for Trees.

A selection of other 'opinionated guides' to London

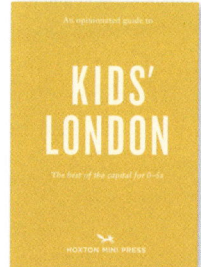

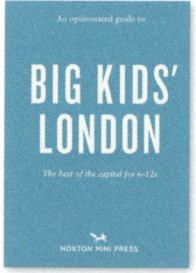

For more go to www.hoxtonminipress.com

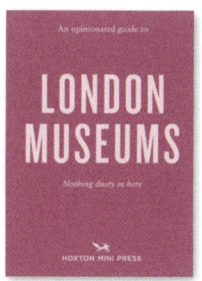

IMAGE CREDITS

Planque © Anton Rodriguez; Cadet © Sam A. Harris; Hector's © Charlie McKay; Bar Levan © Nic Crilly-Hargarve; Top Cuvée © Maria Bell; Lulu's © Lulu's; Noble Rot © Tom Cockram; Leroy © Helen Cathcart; Cloth © Ed Dallimore; Le Beaujolais © David Post; Gordon's © Paul Marc Mitchell; Lady of the Grapes @ Elio Ruscetta; Winemakers Club © Mike Taylor @miketaylor. photography; Uncorked © David Post; St. JOHN © Sam A. Harris; Le Cordon Bleu Wine Courses © Le Cordon Bleu; Quality Wines © Anton Rodriguez; The 10 Cases © Justin De Souza; Half Cut Market © Caitlin Isola; The Draper's Arms © Orlando Gili; Hector's © Charlie McKay; Cadet © Sam A. Harris; Dan's © Parched Wine; The Cellars © David Post, Trullo Wine Bar © David Post; Shrine to the Vine © Tom Cockram; 107 © David Post; Forest Wines © Forest Wines; Planque © Anton Rodriguez; Joyau © Cassian Gray; Brawn © Helen Cathcart; Sune © Philippa Langley; Sager + Wilde © David Post; Oranj © Ania Smoliakova @aniasmlkv, courtesy of Oranj @oranjwine; Idle Moments © Idle Moments; Renegade © Maria Bell; Top Cuvée © Maria Bell; Gnarly Vines © Maria Bell; Newcomer Wines © Anton Rodriguez; Brat © Jess Henderson; Polentina © David Post; Forza Wine © Sam A. Harris; Elliot's © Hasselbrand; Chez Bruce © David Post; TÓU © Caitlin Isola @ scaitboard; Bar Levan © Nic Crilly-Hargarve; Dynamic Vines © @Dynamic_ Vines; Borough Wines © Steve Hawkins Photography; Bar Daskal © Alex Knowles; Lulu's © Lulu's; Mother Superior © Stewart Capper; Salthouse Bottles © Heter Pubble; Canton Arms © Matt Hickman; Veraison © Bart Price; 40 Maltby Street © Trent McMinn; Blackbook Winery © Maria Bell; Soif © David Post; London Cru © Maria Bell; The Pelican © The Pelican; 10 Greek Street © David Post; Bar Crispin © Sam A. Harris; Vindinista © David Post; Andrew Edmunds © Nick Moore; The London Wine Academy © The London Wine Academy; Berry Bros. & Rudd first image © Rachael Smith, following images © Lesley Lau; Westwell first image © Lesley Lau, following images © Maria Bell; Oxney © Maria Bell; Tillingham © Lesley Lau; Rathfinny © Rathfinny; Durslade © James Malone.

Acknowledgements
Many thanks to Su, Ali, Ally, Alice, Andrew, Fred, Ruby, Dulcie, Guy, Lucinda,
Tom and Robin, without whom I couldn't have possibly drunk enough to take
an 'authoritative' view on things. Thanks, too, to Flo, Martin and Ann at
Hoxton Mini Press for the blissful commission and extremely tolerant edit.
Chin chin to that. *Tom Howells*

An Opinionated Guide to Wine London
First edition
Published in 2024 by Hoxton Mini Press, London
Copyright © Hoxton Mini Press 2024. All rights reserved.
Text by Tom Howells
Editing by Florence Ward
Proofreading by Zoë Jellicoe
Editorial support by Leona Crawford
Thanks to Matthew Young for initial series design.

Please note: we recommend checking the websites listed for each
entry before you visit for the latest information on price, opening times
and pre-booking requirements. The right of Tom Howells to be identified as the
creator of this Work has been asserted under the Copyright, Designs and
Patents Act 1988. No part of this publication may be reproduced, stored in a
retrieval system, or transmitted in any form or by any means, electronic,
mechanical, photocopying, recording or otherwise, without the prior written
permission of the copyright owner.

A CIP catalogue record for this book is available from the British Library.

ISBN: 978-1-914314-77-3
Printed and bound by OZGraf, Poland

Hoxton Mini Press is an environmentally conscious publisher, committed
to offsetting our carbon footprint. This book is 100 per cent carbon
compensated, with offset purchased from Stand For Trees.
For every book you buy from our website, we plant a tree:
www.hoxtonminipress.com

MIX
Paper | Supporting
responsible forestry
FSC® C163799
FSC
www.fsc.org

INDEX

The 10 Cases, *12*

10 Greek Street, *55*

107, *21*

40 Maltby Street, *50*

Andrew Edmunds, *58*

Bar Crispin, *56*

Bar Daskal, *44*

Bar Levan, *41*

Le Beaujolais, *4*

Berry Bros.
  & Rudd, *60*

Blackbook
  Winery, *51*

Borough Wines, *43*

Brat, *35*

Brawn, *26*

Cadet, *16*

Canton Arms, *48*

The Cellars, *18*

Chez Bruce, *39*

Cloth, *3*

Le Cordon Bleu, *10*

Dan's, *17*

The Drapers Arms, *14*

Durslade, *65*

Dynamic Vines, *42*

Elliot's, *38*

Forest Wines, *22*

Forza Wine, *37*

Gnarly Vines, *33*

Gordon's, *5*

Half Cut Market, *13*

Hector's, *15*

Idle Moments, *30*

Joyau, *25*

Lady of Grapes, *6*

Leroy, *2*

London Cru, *53*

The London Wine
  Academy, *59*

Lulu's, *45*

Mother Superior, *46*

Newcomer
  Wines, *34*

Noble Rot, *1*

Oranj, *29*

Oxney, *62*

The Pelican, *54*

Planque, *24*

Polentina, *36*

Quality Wines, *11*

Rathfinny, *64*

Renegade, *31*

Sager + Wilde, *28*

Salthouse Bottles, *47*

Shrine to the Vine, *20*

Soif, *52*

St. JOHN, *9*

Sune, *27*

Tillingham, *63*

Top Cuvée, *32*

TÓU, *40*

Trullo Wine Bar, *19*

Uncorked, *8*

Veraison, *49*

Vindinista, *57*

Westwell, *61*

Winemakers Club, *7*

Wingnut, *23*